MY BOOK OF
REPTILES

Illustrated by Helen Haywood

The Pied Piper Library
PURNELL
London, W.1

THE GREEN LIZARD *(Lacerta Viridis) 16″ to 24″ long*

Lives along the Mediterranean coast, from Persia to Portugal, and up as far as the Channel Islands. It lives on insects, slugs and worms. A bold lizard, it has been known to attack and kill such dangerous snakes as the Adder. In spring, the Green Lizard lays from 8 to 12 white eggs, which are buried in the sand and hatch in the warmth of the sun, in about 30 days. It is often kept as a pet in outdoor reptiliaries.

THE ADDER *(Vipera Berus) 2′ to 2′ 8″ long*

Ranges from Britain, through Europe to N. Asia and Japan. The only poisonous reptile in Britain, the Adder likes to sun itself on sandy heaths, hillsides and banks. There is a marked variation in colour, the females being larger and generally redder. Adders hibernate through the winter in burrows or holes, several snakes often sharing the same den, appearing about March or April, when they seek their mates. The young—5 to 20—are born alive in the autumn. Mice, voles, frogs, small lizards and slugs are eaten by adults, while the young feed on insects and small worms.

THE COMMON CHAMELEON *(C. Chameleon) up to 2′ long*

This well-known member of the lizard family may be found living along the Mediterranean, from Spain to Palestine, and the north coast of Africa. It is famous for its ability to change colour (though the range of colour is much exaggerated) as well as for its long, sticky-tipped tongue, which is flicked out at lightning speed to catch the insects that are its main food. Another interesting thing about chameleons is their eyes; these are enclosed in thick lids, so that only a pinhole is left through which they see. Each eye can move independently and roll round in a complete circle. The feet, which look like tongs, are used for grasping branches, while the tail acts as a fifth hand. In the spring the female comes down to the ground and digs a hole in which she lays her eggs.

EUROPEAN POND TORTOISE *(Emys Orbicularis) 8″ along shell*

Lives in ponds and streams in south and east central Europe. Here, during the day, it likes to bask in the sun on banks or logs, returning to the water at sunset to spend the night hunting fish, newts, worms and water insects. In eating fish, the Pond Tortoise rejects the fish's air bladder, which then floats to the surface. The sight of these on the water is a sure sign of the presence of Pond Tortoises. On May nights the females come ashore to lay their eggs in holes dug in the banks. Usually 9 to 15 eggs are laid and carefully covered with earth. As winter approaches the Pond Tortoise digs an underground chamber and retires in it until the following spring.

THE FLYING LIZARD *(Draco Volans) 8″ long*

In the Malay Peninsula and the islands of Java, Sumatra and Borneo, live several species of Flying Lizards, the best known of which is Draco Volans, the Flying Dragon. Like some gay butterfly, it glides from tree to tree by means of several elongated ribs, which are covered in flexible skin. When at rest, the 'wings' fold up like a fan, and the mottled green of its back makes it almost invisible on moss-covered tree trunks. The Draco catches insects in flight and only comes to the ground to lay its 3 or 4 white eggs in the forest mould.

THE KOMODO DRAGON *(Varanus Komodoensis)*
10 feet long

On the island of Komodo, and a few nearby islands, lives the largest Monitor lizard in the world. It was discovered in 1915 and with its huge black, sinister look, reminds one of the long-extinct dinosaurs. It is a fierce hunter of pigs and small deer and will also eat carrion. The Dragon lives in rocky dens by night and prowls through the long grasses by day, flicking its purple forked tongue by the means of which it scents the trail of its prey.

THE CROCODILE *(Crocodylus Niloticus) up to 16′ long*

The large rivers and freshwater lakes of Africa are the homes of the Nile Crocodile. Once worshipped by the Ancient Egyptians who, in their temples, adorned it with bangles and rings. At death, these crocodiles were mummified and entombed with honour. Crocodiles live on fish and any unwary animal that comes down to the water to drink. They spend a lot of time sunbathing on sandbanks, often with their jaws open, while the little Nile Plovers run in and out unharmed, cleaning the great reptile's teeth. Crocodiles lay their eggs in a hole dug in a sandbank, the mother staying nearby to keep away the ever hungry Nile Monitors. When the babies are ready to hatch, they make a peeping noise, and the mother scratches away the earth to let out the little crocodiles.

SAVANNA MONITOR *(Varanus Exanthematicus)*
3' 6" long

This Monitor Lizard inhabits the cliffs and rocky hillocks of south and south-east Africa, where it is often seen lying stretched out on a flat rock in the sun. Because it will raid chicken runs, the farmers shoot them as pests, but usually it moves too fast to be caught. Unlike most other lizards, Monitors cannot snap off their tails to avoid capture, and in this way resemble snakes. Another feature shared with serpents, is the long forked tongue, which is constantly flicked in and out. Its usual food consists of small animals and birds' eggs. Their own leathery-shelled eggs, as with many other reptiles, are buried in the ground and left to hatch in the heat of the sun.

PUFF ADDER *(Bitis Arietans) 3' 4" long*

The Puff Adder is the commonest of the African vipers, as well as one of the most poisonous—its bite will kill a rat in a few seconds—so it is greatly feared. Puff Adders live in open country from South Africa to the Sahara, as well as in Morocco and Arabia. The name 'Puff' comes from the habit it has of taking in air, when annoyed, and blowing up its body. Puff Adders produce as many as 70 live young at one time. The little snakes shed their first skins soon after they are born, when they are equipped with poisonous fangs and ready to feed on mice. The adults eat rat-like mammals and hares.

THE GILA MONSTER *(Heloderma Suspectum) 1' 8" long*

This is one of the only two poisonous lizards in the world and is sometimes known as the 'Beaded Lizard', from the rounded shape of its scales. Found in the Southern States of America, it rests in burrows or under rocks by day, coming out at night to feed on young rodents, nest-birds and their eggs. Slow moving and clumsy, it follows its prey by scent. When well fed, the Gila stores fat in its tail, which becomes very plump. Gilas lay from 6 to 12 eggs in the sand. These take about 30 days to hatch.

THE RED-EARED TERRAPIN, or ELEGANT SLIDER *(Pseudemys Scripta Elegans)*

One of a common group of Turtles that have a very ancient past, their ancestors appearing 200,000,000 years ago, before the Dinosaurs evolved. Found in the Mississippi valley, they inhabit quiet backwaters of streams and ponds, spending their days sunbathing on logs or sandbanks. They feed on plants as well as fish and water insects. In June and July the mother turtle digs a vase-shaped hole near water with her hind feet, and in it lays 9 to 23 eggs which take 10 weeks to hatch. In winter the Turtles hibernate under the water, absorbing air through their skins.

THE CORN SNAKE *(Elaphe Gutta) 4′ long*

One of the most beautiful of serpents in the Southern States of America is the Corn Snake. Harmless to man and a friend of the farmer, the Corn Snake keeps the fields and barns free of rats and mice. It is a good climber and will sometimes go up trees in search of birds' eggs and nestlings. The young hatch from eggs laid in rotten wood and tree stumps.

THE MARINE IGUANA *(Amblyrhyncus Cristata Var.) 5′ long*

This is the only sea-going lizard in the world, and one of a group living on the volcanic islands off the coast of South America, known as the Galapagos, or Turtle Islands. The one shown here is from Hood Island. In spite of their fierce appearance, these lizards are quite harmless and never attack other animals. They feed entirely on seaweed growing on the sea floor, and their ability to stay down may be due to the habit of swallowing stones. When annoyed they blow vapour from their nostrils, just like miniature dragons. In January, the males engage in fierce mock battles for the favour of their mates. The female lays her eggs in the dusty soil, buries them and then mounts guard over them, to prevent the others from digging them up.

KIDNEY-TAILED GECKO *(Nephrurus Laevis)* 7" long

Geckos are some of the most attractive of all the lizards, with their soft skin and big eyes. They also have wheezy high-pitched voices, quite startling in a reptile. The Kidney-tailed Gecko lives in the desert parts of Australia, and its large eyes show it to be nocturnal. These eyes have no lids, but the little creature wipes off the dust and dirt with its long tongue. As with other lizards, its tail breaks off, if handled roughly, but it will grow a new one. Sometimes as many as three tails will grow out of the old stump. Geckos lay their eggs under stones or bark and these may take many months to hatch.

THE JEWELLED GECKO *(Diplodactylus elderi)* 4" long

Another charming little lizard that lives among the prickly blades of porcupine grasses, and is found all over the desert regions of Australia. There are some 60 species of Geckos in Australia alone, many doing useful service to man by coming into houses and eating up unwanted insects and spiders.

THE BLUE-TONGUED SKINK *(Tiliqua Scincoides)*
2' long

Skinks belong to one of the two largest families of lizards in the world. Most have rather feeble legs and some have none at all. They spend a good deal of time burrowing underground. The Blue-tongued is the largest of the Skinks and, when alarmed, it flattens its body and displays a wide blue tongue. Snails, insects, small birds, mushrooms, fruit and leaves make up its diet and 12–15 live babies are born at a time.

THE MOLOCH *(Moloch Horridus) 8" long*

In some parts of Australia these lizards are also known as 'Mountain Devils', and in spite of their fearsome appearance, this is unfair. The Moloch is a harmless little creature, living entirely on ants which it licks up with a lightning flick of the tongue. Anything up to 5,000 ants at a time makes a Moloch's meal! It has the power of changing colour, from orange to grey, though not as quickly as the chameleon. It lives in dry sandy places and has the habit of half-burying itself in the sand. Its large eggs, almost an inch long, are hatched in the sand.

THE SAND GOANNA *(Varanus Gouldi)* 6′ long

Goanna is the Australian name for the Monitor Lizards that inhabit that continent and is a corruption of the word Iguana.

Next to the Komodo Dragon, Australia has the largest Monitor Lizards in the world, some of them growing up to 8 feet in length. The 6 foot Sand Goanna is a common species, living successfully in desert, bush and wooded country. It darts about, poking its long tongue into burrows and holes in search of snakes, lizards and small mammals. If the burrow is inhabited, the Goanna digs down furiously with its long claws, from which there is little escape. Male Goannas fight with teeth and claws, lashing out at each other with their tails—tails strong enough to knock a man down or even break a bone. Goannas live in burrows and lay their eggs in holes in the ground.